D1234473

FIFTY SHADES OF GREEN

A STOCK MARKET GUIDE FOR THE FINANCIALLY INDEPENDENT-MINDED WOMAN

RAMAT OYETUNJI

Publisher's Note

This publication is designed to provide accurate information
with regards to the subject matter covered. It is sold with the
understanding that the publisher is not engaged in
rendering financial, legal, or other professional services.
If expert assistance or counseling is needed, the services
of a competent professional should be sought.

Published by Tinu Publishing, LLC

Editing by Indie Author Counsel

Cover design by James, GoOnWrite.com

EBook ISBN-13: 978-0-9863204-1-5

Print B&W ISBN-13: 978-0-9863204-2-2

Print Color ISBN-13: 978-0-9863204-0-8

DEDICATION

To my daughter, who is confident, self-assured and teaches me something new and interesting every day.

INSIDE FIFTY SHADES OF GREEN

Introduction   1

Chapter 1: Saying Hello to Your Future Self   11

Chapter 2: Getting to the Heart of the Matter   17

Section 1: The Stock Market, Stock Exchanges
and Brokerage Firms   17

Section 2: Stocks   25

Section 3: Bonds   33

Section 4: Mutual Funds   44

Section 5: Stock Market Indices   50

Chapter 3: Making Money & Reducing Risk   57

Chapter 4: Taking Control & Keeping It   75

ACKNOWLEDGMENTS

My husband, for his constant support and sounding board role. My parents, Dr. & Mrs. A.A.A. Oyetunji, for the solid foundation they provided me. My Oyetunji siblings and San Diego sibling, who are an endless source of encouragement and provide proofreading services. Fellow author and mentor, Tope Ganiyah Fajigbesi. Roger Harris and Diane Koerner, for their editing services and objective feedback. Finally, Dr. Robert Strong, whose Investment Banking class cemented my love for investing.

"You gain strength, courage and confidence by every experience in which you really stop to look fear in the face."

— Eleanor Roosevelt

INTRODUCTION

In **Fifty Shades of Green,** you will not find Christian Grey or indulge in erotic fantasies. What you will find is financial information that will empower you to fulfill some of your financial fantasies. For instance:

* ❖ Your fantasy of breaking free from the shackles that bind you to a desk, a job or a place. (These shackles are not the sexy kind!)

* ❖ Your fantasy of having the time to enjoy your friends, kids, grandkids, spouse, and other relatives, and being there when they need you the most.

* ❖ Your fantasy of controlling your own destiny and being master of your universe, without money being your number one constraint.

* ❖ Your fantasy of being able to support and champion the causes nearest and dearest to your heart.

These are some of my financial fantasies, and I suspect other women share them as well. I am making my fantasies a reality, and I want to share one way of doing that with other women. You can stop fantasizing and start turning your fantasies into reality through financial knowledge and planning; specifically, gaining knowledge about investing in the stock market.

Have you heard of the confidence gap?

(Illustration by Edmon de Haro)

Katty Kay and Claire Shipman in their book, *The Confidence Code*, identified a "confidence gap" among women that seemed to hold them back. This confidence gap is evident in the way women manage their finances.

Today, women are more financially powerful than ever before, but our nest egg does not reflect our success. One reason is that we are less confident investors and thus, less willing than men to take risks. We are lagging behind when it comes to investing and planning for our future. Fewer women than men seek financial knowledge, fewer women than men open investment accounts and when we do open investment accounts, women are less likely than men to review their investments.

It does not have to be that way. The information that I provide in this book will increase your financial knowledge and investing confidence. In the book, I arm you with practical steps to spur you into action. Every action that you take regarding the planning of your financial future will increase your confidence and spur further action.

Figure 1: How Would You Rate Your Financial Knowledge?

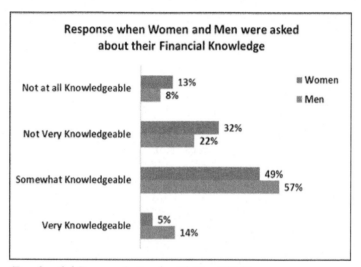

(Prudential Research Study, 2012 - 2013)

This book focuses on improving financial knowledge by learning the basics of investing in the stock market. I have written it for women because educating women, and improving our financial knowledge, is near and dear to my heart. I am focusing on the stock market because for long term investing, it is one of the best ways to grow your money and stay ahead of inflation. I will explain more about what the stock market is and the impact inflation has a little further in the book.

I want to use this book to move the 45% of women in the "Not at all Knowledgeable" and "Not Very Knowledgeable" categories, into the "Somewhat Knowledgeable" category, and eventually into the "Very Knowledgeable" category. I want to inspire other women and fuel a movement of Financially Independent Women.

Let me begin by sharing a little bit about me, and my journey to improve my own Financial Knowledge. I have 15 years of experience as an investor, and I was a licensed Financial Advisor. I have always been passionate about financial freedom, and in my quest, I have experienced many of the stages that investors go through. I have progressed from "Not Very Knowledgeable" to "Very Knowledgeable" and have learned valuable lessons about the stock market and investing along the way.

During one of the early stages of my journey, when I was still "Not Very Knowledgeable", I fooled myself into thinking that I could use the stock market to get rich quickly. Without taking the time to understand the stock market or the various factors that determine a sound investment, I jumped into investing headfirst. I was so convinced that investing as much money as possible in one or two "hot" stocks would get me rich quickly, that I went as far as borrowing money to invest. As you may have already guessed, I made several ill-advised investments and lost what little bit of money I had. *I now know that understanding how my investments work makes me a better investor.*

Another stage occurred a few months after September 11, 2001. There was still a lot of confusion and fear in the country. Many US companies were suffering from the aftermath of the events of 9/11, which resulted in the lay-off of many employees. I was one of those unfortunate employees. I felt the same uncertainty and fear that everyone else felt, and it made me very risk averse. This risk aversion led me to put what little money I had in a savings account, vowing never to set foot in the stock market again because I was afraid I would lose it all. I became ultra conservative and spent some time sitting on the sidelines, afraid to invest in the stock market. However, with interest rates below 1%, my money was barely growing and definitely not growing with inflation.

As a Financial Advisor, I learned firsthand about all the different stages that investors go through; from the fear of losing all their money, to the thrill of thinking that they will become rich overnight.

I had the opportunity to work with "regular" investors. People who were not experts and just wanted their money to help them achieve goals like sending their kids to college, enjoying a nice vacation with friends and family, and retiring when they chose. The common theme amongst these investors was that they did not understand the stock market, and as humans, we tend to fear and avoid what we do not understand.

Why focus on the Stock Market?

For long term investing, the stock market provides the best opportunity for you to grow your money and stay ahead of inflation, and requires very little initial investment. Compared with starting a business or buying real estate, anyone can begin investing in the stock market with as little as $50.

The other reason to focus on the stock market is that it touches almost every aspect of our daily lives. It could impact you through your (or your spouse/partner's) retirement plan, pension plan, mortgage/rent, car loan, or your savings account with a bank or credit union. The stock market can even have an impact on your employment status, if companies are unable to raise money for expansion and further development. I will go into detail about these and other aspects of the stock market, in the chapters to come.

Since the stock market plays an important role in our lives, why are so few people "Very Knowledgeable" about it? The simple answer is that the stock market can be complex and sometimes the "experts" make it even more complicated by using a lot of technical and trade jargon. No wonder people immediately assume that the stock market is too complicated and either avoid it, or underutilize it.

My goal is to explain the basics of investing in the stock market in simple language, using everyday imagery and relating it to the way we women interact. We are conversational and we learn best from experience and sharing that experience with others. I will present important concepts using examples as we follow you and a fictitious friend around the mall one weekend.

If a woman is on the sidelines and not investing in the stock market, I want it to be because of an educated decision that she made, and not because of a "confidence gap."

What will you learn from this book?

After reading this book, you will know common investing terms, and have a better understanding of how to invest your money. I will arm you with simple steps for taking and keeping control of your financial future.

Before proceeding, ask yourself:

How would I rate my Financial Knowledge?

    ☐   Not at all knowledgeable

    ☐   Not very knowledgeable

    ☑   Somewhat knowledgeable

    ☐   Very knowledgeable

"Controlling your own destiny is fun"

— *Queen Latifah, Businesswoman & Entertainer*

CHAPTER 1

SAYING HELLO TO YOUR FUTURE SELF

"Hello, Mary. I hope you are having a wonderful day. Your account balance is $75,016" said an electronic voice over the phone.

Mary stared at the screen of her phone for a moment. She always had a moment of reflection when one of her bank apps told her the balance in that particular account. She confirmed the amount she had just heard and smiled. She could not have dreamed 30 years ago that the monthly $50 investment that her father insisted she make when she started her first summer job would amount to so much. At the time, she grudgingly did it to please him, but it soon became automatic; a habit that she never broke. She paused again, and gave silent thanks to her father.

The benefit of investing in the stock market lies in being able to grow your money and beat inflation. It is one way to ensure that your money outlives you, instead of the other way around. Author, Lance Drucker, shares a story from his book, *How to Avoid Bag Lady Syndrome*, where he

11

recalls a wealthy woman telling him that her biggest fear was running out of money and "becoming a bag lady." If you do not grow your money, and grow it faster than inflation, the fear of outliving your money becomes a reality.

In the beginning of the chapter, you learned that Mary put aside $50 every month when she started her first summer job. It was the first thing she did when she received her paycheck. At first, she did it reluctantly and only to please her father since he had been so insistent. She especially did not enjoy telling her friends that she had to skip going to the movies, or meeting for lunch because she had to set aside $50 every month, but she did tell them, and she did set aside $50 every month without fail.

After a few months of setting aside $50 from her paycheck, she started budgeting based on what was left of her paycheck after the $50 deduction, and after a while, she no longer even thought of the $50 she set aside every month. It was something she did automatically. The $50 had become invisible to her!

The rest, as they say, is history. Thirty years later, Mary's monthly $50 investment had grown to $75,016!

If Mary had stuffed her monthly $50 under her mattress, she would have $18,000 to show for it, instead of $75,016. If she had kept the money in a savings account for 30 years, she would have $37,280[1] instead of $75,016[2]. Neither amount comes close to the purchasing power of her current balance of $75,016!

As you read this book, you will learn about different investments and the strategies that Mary used to grow her money.

For long term investing, the stock market provides the best opportunity for you to grow your money, and stay ahead of inflation. We have already seen from Mary's example how your money can grow, but what does inflation have to do with it?

If I had a penny for how many times I have heard someone say, "In my day, you could get a cup of coffee for 5 cents," I could probably retire rich!

Kidding aside, Inflation causes the price of goods and services to rise. Due to inflation, if Mary had kept her money under her mattress, its value would decline yearly, because what she could buy with the money she saved would get smaller every year.

---

[1] Average savings interest rate of 4.08% from 1984 to 2014

[2] S&P 500 Annualized rate of return of 8.3% from 1984 to 2014 with dividends reinvested. Trading fees not taken into account.

Figure 2: Illustration of the effect inflation has on $5,000 over 10 years

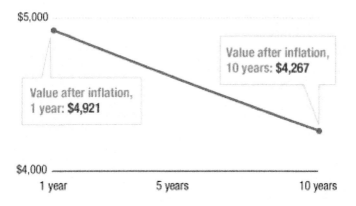

CHAPTER SUMMARY

So far, you have learned that:

❖ The stock market is one of the best ways to grow your money and beat inflation.

❖ The stock market affects you even when you think you have nothing to do with it.

❖ Inflation reduces the value of money over time.

Before you proceed, ask yourself:

☐ How would an extra $40,000 help you turn some of your fantasies into reality?

Mary was able to gain almost $40,000 more by investing in the stock market instead of a savings account.

"A Woman's best protection is a little money of her own"

— *Clare Boothe Luce, former American Ambassador.*

CHAPTER 2

GETTING TO THE HEART OF THE MATTER

Section 1: The Stock Market, Stock Exchanges and Brokerage Firms

What is the stock market?

One lovely weekend afternoon, you and your girlfriend, Kelly, decide to go to the mall. It is one of those outside malls, and since it has been raining for the past couple of days, you think there is no better way to enjoy the day than to indulge in a little outdoors shopping. You do not have anything specific to buy, you are really just planning to browse and spend time with Kelly, but if you come across a bargain, you will not pass it up. The mall you are going to is a large one, with many stores selling items ranging from discount clothes, high-end fashion, high-tech gadgets to children's toys and home decorations. Some of the stores sell only unique or novelty items and other stores have a wide variety of items that appeal to a range of people. At the mall, there is something for everyone, every style, budget, and taste.

Think of the **stock market** like your neighborhood mall. It is a place where **brokerage firms** trade (buy and sell) **securities (investment instruments like stocks, bonds and mutual funds)**. Just like your neighborhood mall, the stock market has operating hours. For the U.S. stock market, the operating hours are from Monday to Friday from 9:30 a.m. to 4:00 .pm. Eastern Standard Time. The stock market is closed on major holidays.

Figure 3: Imagine the Stock Market as your neighborhood mall

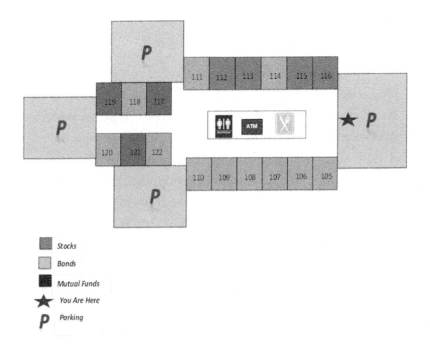

As you wander through the mall, you stop at one of your favorite stores. You love shopping there because you enjoy looking through the racks of clothes, looking at the different brands, and doing your own research on the quality and value of the items. You know what you like, and you have some experience or recommendations to rely on when selecting the items you want. You do not like the stores where a sales person is constantly hovering and asking you if you need help, or constantly trying to steer you to a particular item. While you are shopping, if you have a question about a particular item, you will find a salesperson. You do not mind waiting, and you do not mind that they have limited knowledge; you have already done your own research anyway.

Kelly on the other hand does not like stores where she has to rifle through racks of clothes. She does not enjoy spending time searching or researching the different brands and styles in order to find the one that best meets her needs. Instead, Kelly would prefer to receive guidance through the process of selecting a brand and style. Hence, she heads to her favorite store at the mall where she has an assigned personal shopper/assistant. This person helps her determine the best items to buy by asking her questions and offering recommendations based on her answers. Kelly loves it. She prefers to rely on the knowledge of her assigned personal shopper to steer her in the right direction with minimal or no research on her part. Understandably, there are costs associated with this type of service. In the end, you both enjoy the experience and usually leave satisfied.

Brokerage Firms

Think of brokerage firms as similar to the stores in the mall. They buy and sell goods (securities) in the stock market. An example of a brokerage firm is Fidelity Investments.

Just like the stores in the mall, some brokerage firms offer a narrow selection of investments that appeal to a few investors, while others offer a wide range of investments that appeal to a majority of investors. There are brokerage firms that allow you to manage your account by yourself and are typically discount firms, while other brokerage firms are full service firms where you have a financial advisor that manages your account for a fee. Some brokerage firms offer both discount and full service options. Many brokerage firms are 100% online-based, while others have a website and traditional offices.

As you can see, like the stores in the mall, there are a variety of brokerage firms offering various types of securities and different levels of service. It is up to you to determine the brokerage firm that is right for you. In Chapter 4, I list more examples of brokerage firms along with key information to help you compare firms.

Securities and Stock Exchanges

According to a definition by *Investopedia*, a Security is "A financial instrument that represents an ownership position in a publicly-traded corporation (stock), or a creditor relationship with a governmental body or a corporation (bond)."

Besides stocks and bonds, mutual funds are also securities. Prior to trading in the stock market, a security is listed on a stock exchange. A stock exchange is responsible for the electronic execution of trades, in addition to other functions.

The function of a stock exchange is similar to that of credit card companies. Credit card companies do not own any of the stores in the mall, or any of the items sold in the store; they only process the transactions for a fee that the merchants pay.

Examples of stock exchanges are the **NYSE** (New York Securities Exchange) and the **NASDAQ** (National Association of Securities Dealers Automated Quotations). They are companies in of themselves and exist to perform services required in the processing of securities trading (like Visa® and MasterCard® in the credit card analogy).

The size of a company drives its listing on a Stock Exchange. Most securities are listed on stock exchanges, and those that are too small to be listed on an exchange are traded over-the-counter (OTC) on the OTC Bulletin Board (OTCBB).

Examples of companies and the stock exchange they are listed on: Microsoft (listed on the NASDAQ), Verizon (listed on the NYSE), and Blockbuster (OTC).

In this section, you learned that:

❖ The stock market is where securities are traded, and just like the mall, the stock market has hours of operation.

❖ The most common securities traded in the stock market are Stocks, Bonds, and Mutual Funds

❖ Brokerage firms offer various levels of service for managing investment accounts

❖ Securities are listed on Stock Exchanges, and stock exchanges, such as the NYSE, perform transactions involved in securities trades.

Before you proceed, ask yourself:

☐ Would you prefer to do your own research and manage your own account, or are you like Kelly who would prefer to let a financial advisor do the research and manage her account? Maybe a combination of both?

*Let us take a deeper look at securities, starting with **stocks**.*

Figure 4: Your stroll around the mall bring you to the Stocks section

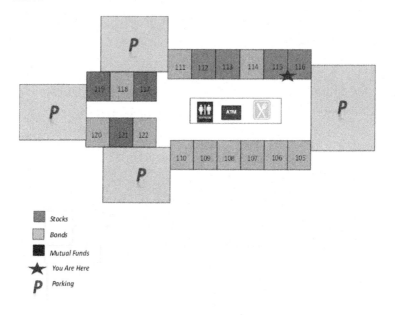

Section 2: Stocks

"I _own_ that company!"

As soon as you arrived at the mall, you and Kelly stopped at the ATM to withdraw some cash. You do all of your banking at a Credit Union. You like supporting the community by banking locally and you like their slogan, "member owned."

When you first joined the credit union, the brochure explained "member owned" meant that all members "own" the credit union and share in its profits. You even noticed that your savings account is a "shares" account. You really like the idea of being a part owner of a local business, the credit union.

A company's stock is its equity or perceived value based on factors such as annual sales, annual profit, current and planned investments or developments, and most importantly, its potential future growth.

Companies capitalize on their equity by offering ownership in the company in the form of share. When you buy shares of a company, you own the company's stock, and you become a part owner of the company. You share in the company's success through stock price appreciation and distribution of profits (through **dividends**). _These are two of the ways that you make money in_ *the stock market. You will learn more about making money in the stock market in Chapter 3.*

"Blue Chip" is a term used to refer to the stocks of companies that are well established, financially stable, and profitable. These companies have been around for a long time and have withstood many challenges. Some examples of blue chip stocks are **Procter & Gamble, Coca-Cola, McDonald's and Walmart**. They offer investors stability and confidence because of their steady growth and consistent dividend payout (the amount of the dividend may vary in a given period depending on the company's profits).

Procter & Gamble, a blue chip company, has paid dividends to investors for 124 consecutive years!

Before trading in the stock market, a company must select the symbol under which it will trade. The symbol, sometimes called ticker, is usually easy to identify with the company, though that is not always the case. For instance, **General Electric's** stock symbol is **GE** and **Facebook's** stock symbol is **FB**. These are easily associated with the companies. On the other hand, **Southwest Airlines'** stock symbol is **LUV**, which is not easily associated with the company, but may resonate with the company's image.

The length of the stock symbol depends on the exchange with which it listed. The NYSE allows symbols up to three letters long (For example, **F for Ford, PG for Procter & Gamble**), while the NASDAQ allows up to five letters (For example, **MSFT for Microsoft**®).

The first time a company offers its stock to the public, it undergoes an Initial Public Offering (**IPO**) during which its initial stock price and the number of shares it will issue to the public are set based on its perceived value or equity. After the company's stock is introduced to the stock market, its price changes as trading begins. Since the stock market operates as a free market where prices are set based on supply and demand, the price of a company's stock will rise and fall based on the demand (people wanting to buy the stock) and supply (shareholders who are willing to sell the stock) .

Facebook's (FB) IPO date was Friday May 18, 2012. Its shares were offered at an initial price of $38 per share. As the stock was bought and sold by investors, it reached a price of $45 per share and at the close of the stock market on its IPO date, it was trading at $38.23 per share. As of December 12, 2014, Facebook is trading at a price of $78 per share. *Note that at some point between the IPO date and December 2014, Facebook shares traded as low as $17.58 per share.*

The number of shares issued by a company is its **outstanding shares.** Its **Market Capitalization** (Market Cap or Cap) is:

Market Cap = Outstanding Shares x Share Price

Since the share price changes throughout the course of the day, a company's Market Cap also changes throughout the day, though not significantly.

Market Cap is used to categorize companies into Large, Mid or Small Cap and can be used as a way to compare companies against an appropriate benchmark. We will discuss benchmarking later in this chapter. An additional use of a company's Market Cap is to provide investors with a way to evaluate the company's value and performance.

For comparison, when you apply for a loan to buy a house, the bank performs an appraisal of the property. If the appraisal (based on predetermined criteria like the size of the house, location, lot size, etc.) returns a value that is lower than the asking price for the house, the bank is unlikely to loan you the money because the house is overpriced.

The same can apply to stock valuation. If a stock has a high Market Cap, but it has low annual sales, very little money invested in assets such as buildings and equipment, no cash in the bank and no significant developments on the horizon, investors may determine that the stock price is too high because the company has nothing to support a high valuation.

A Large Cap company, such as **Facebook**, has a Market Cap of approximately $10 Billion or more (Facebook's

Market Cap on 12/12/14 was $216 Billion). A Mid Cap company, such as **Groupon**, has a Market Cap of approximately $2 Billion to $10 Billion (Groupon's Market Cap on 12/12/14 was $4.2 Billion). A Small Cap company, such as **Ruby Tuesday**, has a Market Cap of approximately $2 Billion or less (Ruby Tuesday's Market Cap on 12/12/14 was $500 Million).

In general, Small Cap companies have more share price volatility than Large Cap and Mid Cap companies, and their stock are riskier investments but with the potential of higher returns to investors.

Figure 5: An illustration of the relationship between risk and potential return. (Illustrative only, not an exact depiction)

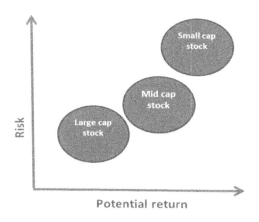

In addition to a stock's Market Cap, another way to evaluate a company is by using its Price to Earnings-Per-Share (**EPS**) ratio or **P/E**.

A stock's P/E is a measure of how "expensive" the stock is when compared to similar stocks. The P/E tells you how much money someone buying the stock has to invest for the company to generate $1 of earnings (profit). The use of a stock's P/E ratio is similar to the "price per unit" used in grocery stores to help shoppers "normalize" the price of similar items.

To illustrate, a company with a share price of $10, and EPS (net income divided by outstanding shares) is $2, then the stock has a P/E ratio of 5. A company's EPS is on its income statement.

When using the P/E ratio to compare stocks, it is important to compare similar stocks. For instance, the stocks should be in similar industries, and have similar Market Capitalization.

P/E and Market Cap are two ways to evaluate stocks; however, you should always take a 360° view to learn about a company. Some other important factors to consider are how long the company has been in existence, changes happening in the company's industry, innovations that the company is developing, to name a few.

In this section on Stocks, you learned:

❖ Owning shares of a company's stock makes you a part owner of the company.

❖ A company first introduces its stock to the market through an IPO (Initial Public Offering).

❖ The length of a company's stock symbol depends on the exchange on which it is listed.

❖ Market Capitalization and P/E are two tools for evaluating stocks and the important of taking a $360°$ view.

❖ The relationship between risk, and potential return for Large Cap, Mid Cap, and Small Cap stocks.

Before proceeding to the next section, ask yourself:

☐ If you had to choose between two companies with P/E ratios of 10, what else would you want to know about each company?

☐ What is Facebook's P/E?

Next, let us look at **Bonds**, *a second type of security.*

31

Figure 6: Your stroll around the mall brings you to the Bonds section

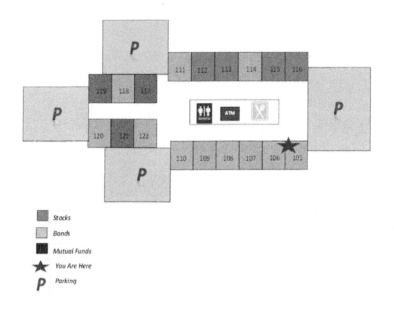

Section 3: Bonds

"I loaned General Electric some money"

The same way you sometimes need to borrow money from the bank to buy a car or a house, companies, and even the government, sometimes need to borrow money to fund various projects. One of the ways they borrow money is by issuing bonds.

While at the mall, you and Kelly stop at the ATM to withdraw some money. You notice that your checking account balance is higher than you were expecting, and after checking the summary on the screen, you realize that the interest from the savings bond your grandmother bought when you were born has been deposited in your account. Just in time for an afternoon at the mall! You have received the interest on a regular basis and will continue receiving it until your 30th birthday. At that time, the initial investment (the face value of the bond) will be returned to you in full. "What a great investment," you think to yourself, as you happily withdraw some of the money.

Bonds are a loan from you to a company, a local government, state government or the federal government. Bonds are a debt obligation of the entity issuing it. In exchange for your loan, interest payments are paid to you at regular intervals, or accrue over the life of the bond, depending on the type of bond.

When you buy a Bond, it will have the following information:

- Issuing entity (e.g. company XYZ)

- Face value/Par value (typically $1000)

- Coupon rate (interest rate)

- Maturity date (the date the face value of the bond is returned to you)

- Issue date (date interest begins to accrue)

- Cusip #(used to identify most securities)

- The bond's rating (similar to a credit score for an individual).

Figure 7: Example of a South Carolina state government bond with a coupon rate of 6%

Bond Rating

When a Bond is issued, it has a rating associated with it. The bond rating, like your credit score, is an indication to investors about the credit quality of the bond and the financial stability of the entity issuing the bond.

Various agencies have different rating nomenclature. The most recognized one is from the Standard & Poor agency. The S&P Bond ratings range from AAA (best) to C (junk). A "D" rating indicates the bond is in default (i.e. payment obligations are not being met). "Investment grade" Bonds are bonds with a rating of BB and higher.

Figure 8: Standard & Poor Bond rating key

AAA	Extremely strong capacity to meet financial commitments. Highest Rating.
AA	Very strong capacity to meet financial commitments.
A	Strong capacity to meet financial commitments, but somewhat susceptible to adverse economic conditions and changes in circumstances.
BBB	Adequate capacity to meet financial commitments, but more subject to adverse economic conditions.
BBB-	Considered lowest investment grade by market participants.
BB+	Considered highest speculative grade by market participants.
BB	Less vulnerable in the near-term but faces major ongoing uncertainties to adverse business, financial and economic conditions.
B	More vulnerable to adverse business, financial and economic conditions but currently has the capacity to meet financial commitments.
CCC	Currently vulnerable and dependent on favorable business, financial and economic conditions to meet financial commitments.
CC	Currently highly vulnerable.
C	Currently highly vulnerable obligations and other defined circumstances.
D	Payment default on financial commitments.

Figure 9: Types of Bonds (Source: Fidelity Investments)

U.S. Treasury	Direct debt obligations issued by the U.S. government, which uses the revenue from the bonds to raise capital and/or make payments on outstanding debt
Agency	Debt obligations issued by agencies of the U.S. federal government or by private agencies, called government-sponsored enterprises (GSEs), which are federally chartered, but publicly owned by their stockholders
Municipal	Debt obligations issued by states, cities, counties, and other public entities that use the loans to fund public projects, such as the construction of schools, hospitals, highways, sewers, and universities
Corporate	Fully taxable debt obligations issued by corporations that fund capital improvements, expansions, debt refinancing, or acquisitions that require more capital than would ordinarily be available from a single lender
High yield	Debt securities rated below investment grade[2] based on the issuer's weaker ability to pay interest and capital, resulting in the issuer paying a higher rate to entice investors to take on the added risk

Bonds from the United States government are some of the safest in the world because they are backed by the full faith of the United States government. In general, government bonds (city, state, federal) are less risky because governments are able to generate income to pay the interest and principal for their bonds by collecting tax revenue.

Bonds are issued in $1000 increments, and the interest is typically paid every 6 months. The months in which interest payments are made, along with other information, are spelled out in the prospectus. The interest payment on a bond is also known as a coupon payment and the frequency of payment is the coupon frequency.

To illustrate, let us say you purchase a bond from Company XYZ with a 5% coupon rate. The bond has a face value of $1,000. The annual interest on the bond is $50 ($1,000 x 0.05). You will receive two payments of $25 each in the months specified in the prospectus.

In the example above, if you paid face value (i.e. $1000) for the bond, then the yield is 5%, the same as the coupon rate.

Yield = Annual Interest / Bond Price x 100

Bond Prices

Most Bonds are traded on the stock market, and do not have to be held until the maturity date. A **Bond Quote** is the price at which a bond is currently trading. The price that an investor is willing to pay for the bond is expressed with respect to the par value. A bond quote above 100 means that the bond is trading above par, while a bond quote below 100 means that the bond is trading below par.

The price of a bond may be different from its par value because of factors such as its due date, rating, and current interest rates. The factor that has the biggest impact on Bond prices is interest rates.

When interest rates rise, the prices of bonds in the market fall, and when interest rates fall, the prices of bonds in the market rise.

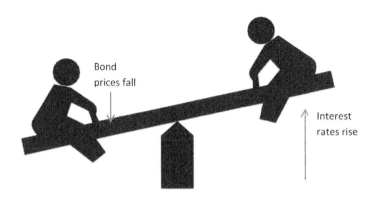

Bond prices fall

Interest rates rise

To illustrate, let us refer to the 5% Bond of company XYZ. If interest rates have risen to 10%, that means you or someone else could potentially buy a 10% bond at face value ($1000) and receive $100 in interest payment annually i.e. a 10% yield. Your XYZ bond has a yield of 5%, and in order to make your bond attractive to a buyer you would have to reduce the price (sell below par) so that the buyer can get a yield of 10%. Remember,

---

Yield = Annual Interest /Bond Price x 100

Since the annual interest never changes, the only thing that can change in the equation is the price. In this case, the price of the XYZ 5% Bond would have to fall to 50 (50% of par). Meaning, someone buying the bond would pay $500 for the bond even though it has a face value of $1000. This would bring the yield to 10% ($50/$500). The lower price makes the XYZ 5% Bond comparable to other bonds selling at par with a 10% coupon rate.

The main advantage of investing in bonds is that your initial investment (principal) remains intact for the specified length of the bond, and you receive predictable interest payments. Bonds are an especially good investment for retirees who do not want to risk the loss of their initial investment.

One of the disadvantages of bonds is that because they are a less risky investment than stocks, their returns are lower over the long run, and since interest payments are fixed, they do not keep up with inflation.

In this section on Bonds, you learned:

❖ Issuing bonds is a way for companies and governments to raise money for various projects and expenses.

❖ A bond's rating is similar to an individual's credit score and provides investors with an indication of the bond's quality and the issuing entity's financial stability.

❖ Important pieces of information to note on a bond are its coupon rate, coupon frequency, maturity date and bond rating.

❖ Bonds can sell above or below face value. The biggest factor influencing bond prices is interest rates.

❖ A bond's yield is determined by its price and can be different from its coupon rate.

Before proceeding to the next section, ask yourself:

☐ What price can you expect to pay for a 10% Bond when the current interest rate is 5%?

Next, let us look at **Mutual Funds**, *the last type of security.*

Figure 10: Your stroll around the mall has taken you to the Mutual Funds section

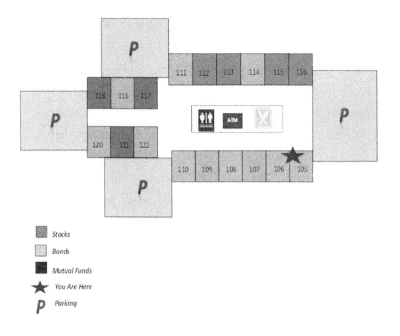

Section 4: Mutual Funds

"Are all my eggs *really* in one basket?"

You have been browsing the mall for a while, and you and Kelly have a number of bags with you. You are tired, but pleased with your purchases. You both decide it is time to take a break, and head towards the food court. As you approach the food court, you walk by one of your favorite spa stores, the one that sells exotic smelling lotions, soaps, candles and a variety of other spa items. You remember that you are almost out of one of your hand lotions and ask Kelly to make a quick stop with you. Although she is starving, she reluctantly agrees to make a quick stop.

As you enter the store, a smiling sales clerk greets you, offering you one of their new signature scents in the form of a body mist. You immediately love it, but it comes in a big bottle and with a price tag that has you doing a double take. The clerk shows you a lotion and body wash with the same lovely scent, and like the body mist, the lotion and body wash each come in large bottles and equally large price tags. You really like the scent and the clerk mentioned that for the best effect, you have to use all three products. You are convinced, but you know that you cannot afford to buy each item. Even Kelly tries to convince you to buy all three items because she had recently bought a similar scent from the store, and she found that using the lotion, wash, and mist together really did make a difference.

You are disappointed but know that you cannot afford all three items, so you start to leave the store. Before you reach the door the sales clerk shows you a basket containing a sample size of the body mist, as well as sample sizes of lotion, soap, and hand cream of the same signature scent. The price for the basket is comparable to that of the big bottle of mist, and since you really, really, like the scent, you decide to buy it. After all, you tell Kelly, you could try other scents if you got tired of this one and you will not be stuck with the big bottles. It seemed less risky.

Figure 11: Think of Mutual Funds like a basket containing individual stocks or bonds

Mutual funds are comprised of various individual securities, usually in a specific sector of the stock market. When you buy shares of a mutual fund, think of it as buying "sample sizes" of the companies that are contained within the mutual fund. It gives you the ability to invest in many companies without having a lot of money.

An example of a Mutual Fund is the **Vanguard Total Market Index Fund**. It consists of 3804 stocks, including stocks of companies like Apple, Google, Procter & Gamble, Microsoft, and Wells Fargo.

Another example of a Mutual Fund is the **Fidelity Select Pharmaceuticals Portfolio**. The Mutual Fund contains the stocks of 85 Pharmaceutical companies. Approximately 50% of the stocks are U.S. based and the other 50% are international stocks. This is one example of an industry specific Mutual Fund with domestic and international exposure.

If you buy one share of either Mutual Fund, you are automatically investing in a variety of companies without having to buy each company's stock.

In addition to providing the opportunity to invest in many companies without having a lot of money, Mutual Funds also offer the opportunity to reduce risk through diversification. Using the Pharmaceutical Mutual Fund to illustrate, if one of the companies in the mutual fund performs poorly, there may be other companies that perform well to offset the poor performance. In this particular example, there is also the added benefit of regional diversification because half the stocks in the Mutual Fund are domestic (US) and the other half are international stocks. If US stocks perform poorly in general, the international stocks may offset the poor performance, thereby reducing your risk. That is the beauty of diversification.

Mutual Fund pricing

The price of a Mutual Fund is determined each business day. A fund's net asset value (NAV) per share is the current value of all the fund's assets (the market value of the underlying securities), minus liabilities (money owed to banks and others), divided by the total number of Mutual Fund shares outstanding.

$$NAV = (Assets - Liabilities)/ \text{\# of outstanding shares}$$

Load or No Load?

One way that Mutual Funds are classified is by their sales charge. A mutual fund without a sales charge is a **No Load** fund and its share price is the same as the NAV. A mutual fund with a sales charge is either a **Front End Load** fund (NAV plus sales fee) or a **Back End Load** fund (shares are purchased at NAV but when sold, a sales charge is imposed. Make sure you read the prospectus to determine how the fees are determined).

To illustrate, imagine you are an investor in XYZ mutual fund, a No Load fund comprised of stocks from two of your favorite companies, Google and Facebook. XYZ mutual fund owns 10 shares of Facebook and 10 shares of Google. The closing share price for Google and Facebook on this particular day was $500 and $75 respectively. This means XYZ mutual fund has **Assets** of $5750. The fund also has a **Liability** of $1000 (money borrowed from a bank for business purposes), and 100 **shares outstanding** (number of shares sold to investors).

XYZ Mutual Fund's NAV for the day is:

NAV = ($5750 - $1000)/100 = $47.50

Since XYZ Mutual Fund is a No Load fund, an investor with $1000 to invest would buy 21 shares of XYZ mutual fund based on the NAV of $47.50 for that day.

Mutual Fund orders are based on the price computed at the end of the trading day (not real-time like stocks), so if an investor buys shares of the fund at 1 pm, the price paid will not be known till after the trading day ends.

In this section on Mutual Funds, you learned:

❖ Mutual funds are like a basket containing various individual securities.

❖ Mutual Funds can help reduce your investment risk through diversification

❖ How Mutual Funds are priced and how they are classified based on the sales charge

Before proceeding to the next section, ask yourself:

☐ What other types of Mutual Funds are there?

☐ What types would interest you?

Next, we will look at **Stock Market Indices**.

Section 5: Stock Market Indices

"It's the twelve days of Christmas"

You and Kelly have finally made it to the food court for lunch; you are famished and cannot wait to dig into the burger you just ordered.

"Do you know what five gold rings cost?" Kelly asks suddenly.

You look at her mystified, and she proceeds to tell you an amusing story from the nightly news the previous day. She said that in the story, the price of each item from the popular Christmas carol "The Twelve Days of Christmas" was determined, and when added up, all the items totaled $27,393.17! She found the story very amusing.

You laugh, telling her that it is the Christmas Price Index and it is calculated by adding up the price of each item from the song; the total price is then compared to the total price from the previous year. It is a tongue-in-cheek gauge for inflation. The official measure for inflation is the government's Consumer Price Index (**CPI**).

"My dad hates seeing the report on the news because the Index is always rising. He said that in 1984 the price of the items was $12,673.56 and in 2013 it was $27,393.17!" you tell Kelly between bites of your burger.

THE TWELVE DAYS OF CHRISTMAS
30 YEARS OF RISING PRICES

TOTAL COST FOR GIFTS IN THE SONG

1984	2012	2013
$12,673.56	$25,431.18	$27,393.17

% CHANGE OVER THE YEARS

2013/12: +7.7%   30 YRS: +116.1%

1984   2013

GIFTS FROM YOUR TRUE LOVE

1 PARTRIDGE IN A PEAR TREE

1984	2012	2013
$32.52	$204.99	$189.99

2 TURTLE DOVES

1984	2012	2013
$47.73	$125.00	$125.00

3 FRENCH HENS

1984	2012	2013
$15.23	$125.00	$165.00

4 CALLING BIRDS

1984	2012	2013
$280.00	$519.96	$599.96

5 GOLDEN RINGS

1984	2012	2013
$325.00	$750.00	$750.00

6 GEESE-A-LAYING

1984	2012	2013
$150.00	$210.00	$210.00

7 SWANS-A-SWIMMING

1984	2012	2013
$7,000.00	$7,000.00	$7,000.00

8 MAIDS-A-MILKING

1984	2012	2013
$28.00	$58.00	$58.00

9 LADIES DANCING

1984	2012	2013
$3,511.78	$6,294.03	$7,552.84

10 LORDS-A-LEAPING

1984	2012	2013
$1,879.75	$4,766.70	$5,243.37

11 PIPERS PIPING

1984	2012	2013
$1,511.78	$6,294.03	$7,552.84

12 DRUMMERS DRUMMING

1984	2012	2013
$934.47	$2,775.50	$2,854.00

 PNC

PNC CHRISTMAS PRICE INDEX.COM

A stock market index is similar to the Christmas Price Index. Instead of measuring inflation, a stock market index tracks the performance of the stock market and is an indicator of economic health.

Think of the stock market index like a basket consisting of stocks from various sectors of the economy, just as the Christmas Price Index consists of items from the Twelve Days of Christmas. The value of a particular index rises and falls as the price of the stocks within the basket rise and fall.

The most common stock indices are the **S&P 500**, the **Dow**, and the **NASDAQ**.

Let us take a closer look at each stock market index.

The Dow - Dow Jones Industrial Average (DJIA)

An index of 30 stocks of U.S. companies, the DJIA includes a wide range of companies—from financial services companies, to computer and retail companies— but excludes transportation and utility companies, which are included in separate indices. The Dow was compiled in the late 1800s to gauge the performance of the industrial sector within the American economy. It gets its name from its creators, Charles Dow and Edward Jones.

Though the index is influenced by economic and political factors, it can be a gauge of the U.S. economic health.

The companies included in the Dow are members of a very elite class. They have withstood the test of time and have proven to be financially stable. If a company does not perform up to the predetermined standards, it is removed from the index if its performance does not improve.

Examples of companies in the Dow: Nike, Procter & Gamble, Walmart, Walt Disney, AT&T, Coca-Cola, Home Depot and McDonald's, the "Blue Chip" stocks mentioned earlier.

S&P 500 – The Standard & Poor's 500 Composite Stock Price Index

The S&P 500 is a frequently used benchmark for individual stock performance, and regarded as the best overall measurement of U.S. stock market performance.

The S&P 500 consists of the stocks of 500 companies, and is a representative sample of leading companies in leading industries within the U.S. economy. These companies are the "who's who" of companies in the U.S. and represent 80% of the market capitalization of the total stock market. The companies are chosen for market size, liquidity (available cash), and industry group representation.

The S&P 500 is a weighted index, and is weighted based on the member companies' outstanding shares. This means that companies with a higher number of outstanding shares have a greater representation and impact on the index.

As of June 2014, the top 10 weighted S&P 500 companies, i.e., the companies with the top 10 largest number of outstanding shares, were Apple, Exxon Mobil, Microsoft, Johnson & Johnson, General Electric, Wells Fargo, Chevron, Berkshire Hathaway, JP Morgan Chase and Procter & Gamble.

The NASDAQ - NASDAQ Composite Index

The Nasdaq Composite Index comprises all of the stocks traded on the NASDAQ Stock Exchange, approximately 3000 U.S. and International stocks. Technology stocks make up approximately 70% of the index; hence, it is often used as a guide for how well technology stocks are doing.

The Nasdaq Index represents a small portion of the total stock market (approximately 30%); hence, it is not as widely used as the Dow and the S&P 500 as a gauge for how the economy is doing.

CHAPTER SUMMARY

In this chapter, you learned:

❖ The stock market is a place where securities are traded

❖ The most common types of securities traded in the stock market are stocks, bonds, and mutual funds.

❖ Securities are listed on Stock Exchanges, which perform trading related services.

❖ How prices for stocks, bonds and Mutual Funds are determined and what influences their prices.

❖ The Dow, S&P 500, and the NASDAQ are indices used to track Stock market performance and US economic health.

"Being rich is having money; being wealthy is having time."

– *Margaret Bonnano, Author of the Star Trek novels.*

CHAPTER 3

MAKING MONEY AND REDUCING RISK

With all that you have learned about the stock market and various securities, how does the stock market get you closer to fulfilling your financial dreams? That is the focus of this chapter.

Making Money in the Stock Market

Money is made in the stock market when the price of a security increases (appreciates), when dividends are paid, or when a coupon payment is made.

We will focus on stock price increases and dividend payments. Bond price movements, and bond interest payments were discussed earlier in the book and Mutual fund prices are dependent on the price of the underlying stocks or bonds they contain.

Price Appreciation

A company's stock price increases when demand for the stock increases because people find the stock attractive and want to own it. As the demand for the stock goes up, its price increases.

Let us look at some of the factors that influence stock price movement.

1. Company Performance

After lunch, you and Kelly head towards your final stop for the day: the shoe store. Right next to your favorite shoe store is the Apple store. You know that Kelly is going to go into the store, and before you have even completed your thought, she is dragging you in.

"Look at the new iPad. Isn't it cool?" Kelly gushes.

You walk over to her and look at the iPad over her shoulders. You admit to yourself that it does look very cool. You look around the store, and as usual, it is full of people browsing the latest Apple gadgets, some of which you did not even know existed. The store has only been open in the mall for a few months, but you are not surprised that it is so popular. You still remember your first visit to the store and how you were very impressed by the many products Apple has, how easy they were to use, and how friendly and knowledgeable the store clerks were. You knew then that the store would attract many people, and you were right. The store has expanded due to its popularity, and it continues to sell a lot of iPads, iPhones, and laptops.

A company is performing well when it sells more products, reduces the cost of making and marketing those products, and generates a larger profit. The company becomes more valuable and so does its stock, which is reflected in an increase of its price. It is typical to see price movement in a company's stock after it reports its quarterly earnings. If its performance is what was expected (or better), the stock price is likely to go up. The reverse also applies.

Opening Apple stores in different malls is one of the ways that Apple shows its investors, competitors and stakeholders that it is expanding its business. The value of the company has increased more than tenfold since a decade ago, because of its increased profits from making new products that people want. Its growth is evident in the creation and expansion of the Apple stores across malls nationwide. The reward to shareholders is an increase in its share price. For example, if you invested $1,000 in Apple stock on January 2 2004, by December 1 2013 your shares would be worth $54,365[3].

---

[3] Based on historical returns from Yahoo finance

2. Perception (or "buzz")

You finally leave the Apple store and head to your favorite shoe store. As you enter the store, you see a pair of shoes that you love. You also notice that they come in different colors. The red pair (the hottest color this fashion season) looks especially stunning, but they are more expensive than the other colors.

"They are the same shoe!" you grumble to Kelly.

"Yes, but red is 'in' this season" she retorts, rolling her eyes.

You both wonder who decided that red was the "in" color. Everyone was talking about the "in" color and it was making every red item more expensive than the other colors. How exasperating!

A company's stock price on a particular day is influenced by the perception of the stock on that day. When "hot" new companies such as Facebook "go public," that is, they start selling shares of their stock on the stock market, the price of the stock may rise based only on the perception that it is a "hot" company generating a lot of interest and attention. Even though the company has yet to demonstrate that it is a reliable investment for investors, the buzz around the company may push its stock price up. The uncertainty surrounding a company that has just gone public is one of the reasons that IPOs are risky investments, and are not suitable for all investors.

3. News about the company's Industry as a whole

You grudgingly pay for the red shoes, but find out 2 weeks later that the same pair of red shoes has been marked down significantly. You remember reading recently that although red is the "must have" color of the season, it must be a particular red called Cherry Blossom. The makers of the red shoes that you bought got the shade of red wrong! Instead of Cherry Blossom, they went with Candy Apple. Although both shoes are of very good quality, the pair you bought is now selling at a discount as fashionistas spread the word that Candy Apple is NOT Cherry Blossom. Too bad, you already paid full price for yours.

A similar situation happens with companies. A company may be in a "hot" industry expected to perform well due to new technology or new consumer trends. The company's stock price may initially increase due to positive expectations about the industry as a whole. However, the price may subsequently decrease, if its product or technology is not what was expected, or is perceived to be different from others in the industry.

4. News or social media mentions (good or bad) about the company

Still fuming about your Candy Apple red shoes, you spot a bag that you and Kelly had previously shunned because you both though it was ugly. The bag was the main feature on a popular fashion show last week, and now you are seeing it in a different, more favorable light. The price of the bag has been marked up 10% from the last time you saw it, and you know it is because of the fashion show.

The stock price for companies can rise or decline in a similar fashion (no pun intended). If a company's product or service is mentioned favorably in a news article, program, blog, or other social media forum, the stock price may rise. If it gets a negative mention, its stock price may fall.

Unless there is a real problem with a company, these price changes are typically temporary. When a stock's price decreases in this manner, it may represent a **"buying opportunity."** News of conflict around the world can also have a negative impact on stock prices if people feel uncertain and start selling their shares.

A real life example occurred with the oil company BP in 2010. BP's stock was negatively impacted after the tragic rig explosion on April 20, 2010. The incident occurred the night of April 20, 2010, and by May 24, 2010, the stock was trading 31% lower than before the incident occurred. Note from the graph how the stock price steadily declines as people become aware of the incident and the magnitude sinks in, the stock becomes less and less attractive.

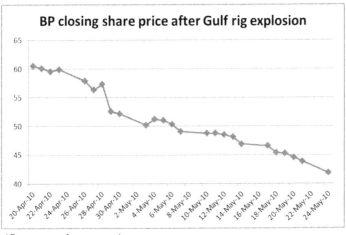

(finance.yahoo.com)

5. Product or service quality

After a week of owning the "ugly" purse, you are dissatisfied with it. The stitching is poor, the clasp has already broken, and the zipper on the inside is stuck. You return to the store to complain and you find that the price of the bag has been marked down even lower than when you originally saw it.

If a company's product or service is poor, its stock price will be negatively impacted no matter how much hype or buzz surrounds the company. As consumers learn about the low quality, they will buy fewer of the company's products or services, which may result in lower profits for the company. With lower profits, the company's stock becomes less attractive to investors.

The same applies to a company with high quality products or services. As consumers learn about the company's high quality products, they buy more of the company's products, which may lead to an increase in products and make the stock attractive to investors.

6. Change in Management

Armed with the cash from the purse you returned, you stop in front of one of your favorite restaurants. You hesitate before going in because you noticed a few weeks ago that your favorite dish no longer tasted the same. Something had changed. You decide to find a new "favorite" restaurant, but feel sad as you walk away. You have good memories of hanging out at that restaurant. You later learn from Kelly that the management of the restaurant changed around the time you noticed a change in the food. Not long afterwards, the restaurant closed.

A change in management can have a big impact on the price of a company's stock. It comes down to investors' uncertainty about how the change will affect the company. Will the change improve the value of the company or worsen its value? Since the main reason for investing in a company is to share in its growth, you expect your investment to grow over time. If the new management inspires confidence, the stock price may be positively impacted. If the new management does not inspire confidence, or there is a noticeable decline in the quality of the products or services, then the stock price may become negatively impacted. Investors may sell their shares in anticipation of the company losing some of its value (as an example, due to loss of customers) and becoming less attractive.

A real life example of this happened after the death of Apple's Steve Jobs. Apple's success was generally attributed to Steve Jobs being at the helm of the company, and investors were concerned that Apple would be a different company under new CEO, Tim Cook's leadership. Apple's stock (AAPL) experienced an initial decline after Steve Jobs' death, but its stock price has since increased as investors gained confidence in Tim Cook.

Let us now look at making money through **dividends**.

Dividends

The first time you shopped at your favorite shoe store, you joined the Shoe Lovers Club and received coupons for discounts that were applicable on your next visit. Ever since then, as a "Thank You for being a Shoe Lover," you have received coupons with significant discounts, in addition to other bargains available in the store. Kelly pointed out that with your discounts, you end up with at least one "free" pair of shoes a year. Your Shoe Lovers Club membership has really paid off.

Think of dividends as a way for a company to "thank you" for investing in its stock. When companies make a profit, they may reinvest all of it in the business in order to grow (for example, they may buy faster equipment or upgrade their technology), or they may distribute all or some of the profit to shareholders in the form of dividends.

Typically, mature companies such as those found in the Dow 30 share a portion of their profit with shareholders and reinvest a portion of the profit. These companies have been paying dividends for many years and are a reliable source of steady income. Earlier in the book, you learned that Procter & Gamble has been paying dividends for 124 years.

Relatively new companies or companies in fast-growing industries typically reinvest all of their profit into the business. These companies tend to experience larger price increases (or decreases) than more mature companies. As an example, prior to 2013, Apple did not pay its shareholders dividends. Instead, it reinvested its profits, and used it for continued research and development of innovative products, which allowed it to grow at a fast pace. Though the shareholders did not receive dividends, the company's growth led to substantial stock price appreciation over time.

Most companies pay dividends every quarter. The company "declares" dividends by announcing a dividend amount per share, the record date, and the dividend payment date. The shareholders on record by the record date will receive a dividend payment. To accommodate the time it takes to record new owners of stocks trades, an "ex-dividend" date is announced and it is the last day investors can buy a company's stock and participate in the dividends for that period.

If you re-invest the dividends you receive by buying more of the company's stock, you are getting "free" shares of the company.

Mutual Funds containing dividend-paying stocks pay a cumulative dividend to shareholders quarterly or annually.

In this section on Making Money, you learned that:

❖ Money is made in the stock market through price appreciation, interest payments (from bonds) and dividends.

❖ Many factors cause a stock's price to rise or fall.

❖ Dividends are a form of reward and a way for investors to share in a company's profits.

Before proceeding to the next section, ask yourself:

☐ What recent news have you heard about companies in your area? How has that news changed your view of those companies?

☐ Have you recently used a product or service that you raved about or that disappointed you? Would you feel confident about investing in such a company?

Reducing Risk

I am sure you have heard the cautionary tale of "putting all your eggs in one basket." **Diversification** reduces investment risk by putting your investment dollars in different "baskets." In the event that something happens to one of your investment "baskets," you have other baskets to rely on. Let us look at a simplified example to show how diversification helps you reduce risk.

Say you invested $100 in company X, a company you greatly admire. Due to some negative news, its stock price drops by 50% and you lose $50 of your investment. However, if you invested $50 in company X and $50 in company Y, and company X has a 50% drop in its share price, you would lose $25 of your investment instead of $50. That is an example of how diversification reduces risk.

There are various ways to diversify your investments, and in order for it to serve the purpose of reducing risk, you should ensure the investments are not similar. For instance, if you invest in two different companies that are in the same industry (e.g., computer manufacturing), the companies' stock prices may decline at the same time because of news or other factors that impact their industry as a whole. It is best to invest in companies that are in different industries and different markets in order to achieve diversification. You can diversify by type of investment (having a mix of stocks and bonds), or diversify by region, country or continent. For instance, if you are invested in 100% U.S. stocks, and the U.S. economy is declining, then your investments may decline as well; however, if you are invested in U.S. and European stocks, and the European economy is faring better than that of the U.S., then your investments will not suffer as much.

Two important factors to consider when determining how to reduce risk are your **risk tolerance** and your **timeline**.

Risk Tolerance and Timeline

Your shopping preferences, such as where you shop and what you buy are driven by your personality, and the same applies when it comes to investing. Your personality plays a role in how you invest and the investments that you select. You will invest differently if you have a high tolerance for risk compared to a low tolerance for risk. The other factor is how much time you have before you need the money invested. The longer you have before you need the invested funds, the more risk you can tolerate because you have time recover from any adverse conditions or affect to your investments.

To illustrate how important time is when making investing decisions, it took five and a half years for the S&P 500 to return to its October 9 2007 level after the

2008 stock market crash. If you had planned to retire during those five and a half years, your investment balance would be lower than if you planned to retire in 10 years (giving your investments time to recover).

How would you respond if you checked your investment account and discovered that your balance had dropped by 20% overnight?

Response 1 – You would most likely take a deep breath and would not react right away because you are confident in your investment selection. Instead, you make a plan to continue monitoring your account without making immediate changes, and even consider buying more shares.

Response 2 – You would most likely panic and would toss and turn all night thinking about the huge drop your account just experienced. You begin to second-guess your investment selections and make plans to sell as soon as the market opens.

If you favor Response 1, you likely have a high tolerance for risk (aggressive), and if you favor Response 2, you likely have a low tolerance for risk (conservative).

Combining your risk tolerance with your timeline gives you your risk profile.

Below is a fun way to think of your risk profile. There is no hard and fast rule around determining your risk profile, and your profile may change as your life changes.

Figure 12: What heel represents your risk profile?

Keep in mind that your investment risk profile may be very different from your fashion style! We will discuss how to use your risk profile in the next chapter.

In this section on Reducing Risk, you learned that:

❖ Diversification is one of the best ways to reduce your risk when investing in the stock market.

❖ Diversification can be by industry, region, investment type, or a combination of other factors.

❖ Important factors for reducing risk are your risk tolerance and timeline. Together they help determine your risk profile.

Before leaving this section, ask yourself:

☐ What is your risk profile?

"People don't take opportunities because the timing is bad, the financial side unsecure. Too many people are overanalyzing. Sometimes you just have to go for it."

– Michelle Zatly, Co-founder of SoundFlare

CHAPTER 4

TAKING CONTROL AND KEEPING IT

Now that you are armed with all this great information, what should you do with it? Take action! Do not procrastinate. Here are some strategies to adopt.

Budgeting

You may be thinking, "I don't have any extra money to set aside." I suggest you make a budget, and take a closer look at where you are spending money. Pay very close attention to your discretionary spending (money left over after you have paid for necessities). Learn to distinguish between "want" and "need." Some places I would suggest looking are your cable bill, cell phone bill, and entertainment expenses (movies and dining out). I "cut the cord" in 2007 by discontinuing cable TV service, and it reduced our family expenses by $60 a month, or $720 a year.

I encourage you to do whatever it takes to budget a monthly amount for investing. Your future self will thank you. Visit my website **www.thefiwoman.com** for a simple, easy-to-use budgeting tool.

Paying yourself first

At the beginning of this book, you were introduced to Mary who managed to invest $50 monthly for 30 years and turned it into $75,016. One of the strategies that Mary adopted was to **pay herself first.**

"Pay Yourself First" is a tried and true strategy. Start by budgeting $50, $100, $500 monthly for investing and have that money withdrawn from your check or account. You will not miss the money if you never even see it. After a while, you will automatically plan your spending without including the $50 or whatever amount you budget.

Making Investing Automatic

Your next step is to **"make investing automatic."** Start with a mutual fund or ETF that tracks the S&P 500 and a bond mutual fund that tracks the total bond market. ETF stands for Exchange Traded Fund. They are similar to mutual funds because they are comprised of various stock or bonds, but unlike mutual funds, they are traded and priced real-time like individual stocks.

A mutual fund that tracks a stock or bond index is called an Index fund. The mix of stocks and bonds you invest in depends on the amount of risk that you are willing to take. As discussed earlier in the book, bonds offer stability, but potentially lower returns, while stocks offer the potential for higher returns but do not have the stability of bonds.

The table below is a simple guide that you may find useful, based on your risk profile. It is a general guide and you should make adjustments as you learn more about your investing style and risk tolerance. In addition, many retirement plans offer Target Funds that automatically determine your investment mix based on the year you plan to retire.

Figure 13: A simple guide for stock and bond mix

Risk Profile	Stocks	Bonds
Stilleto	80%	20%
Kitten heels	60%	40%
Wedge heels	40%	60%
Flat/No heel	20%	80%

Figure 14: Examples of ETF and Index Funds that track the S&P 500

Symbol	IVV	SPY	VOO	VFINX	FUSEX
Security Type	ETF	ETF	ETF	Index Fund	Index Fund
Gross Expense Ratio	0.07%	0.11%	0.05%	0.17%	0.10%
Min Initial Investment	1 share	1 share	1 share	$3,000	$2,500

Figure 15: Examples of ETFs that track the Total Bond Market

Symbol	BND	BOND	SCHZ	FBND	IUSB
SecurityType	ETF	ETF	ETF	ETF	ETF
Gross Expense Ratio	0.08%	0.56%	0.06%	0.45%	0.17%
Min Initial Investment	1 share	1 share	1 share	1 share	1 share

A Word on Fees and Expense Ratios

It is important to pay close attention to the fees incurred during investment activities, because they reduce the return on your investment, i.e., the gains or profit made by your investments.

When you buy or sell individual stocks or ETFs, you incur a trading fee per transaction. The fee charged differs from brokerage firm to brokerage firm. Most online trade fees are under $10 per transaction. Using a financial advisor in person or over the phone will incur premium charges.

To illustrate, if you buy 10 shares of Facebook (FB) at a price of $50 per share using a brokerage firm that charges a fee of $7.95, the total amount processed from your account is $507.95. To get a return on your investment, your investment would have to increase by more than 1.6% ($7.95/$500). If the shares increase by 8% in one year, your actual Return on Investment (ROI) would be 6.4% (8% - 1.6%).

For mutual funds with a sales charge, the sales charge is included in the price of the mutual fund and is incurred when you buy shares (front-end load funds) or when you sell shares (back-end load funds). The sales charge will have the same effect on your return as described in the trading fee example above.

In addition to the sales charge, mutual funds and ETFs have expense ratios. The expense ratio represents the portion of the total assets that is spent on expenses like management fees, administrative fees, etc.

Since ETFs and Index Funds track a specific index and contain the same stocks or bonds that the index contains, they have low expense ratios because they do not need to be actively managed. Actively managed funds have higher expenses because they have managers who decide what stocks or bonds the fund should contain, and monitor their performance closely to determine which ones to sell or buy.

The expense ratio of an ETF or mutual fund has the same effect on your investment return as described in the trading fee example.

To reduce the impact of fees, you may consider accumulating your monthly investment in your brokerage account before buying an investment. A general rule is to aim for less than 1% in fees; lower is better. Note that many ETFs have expense ratios of less than 0.1%.

Get Started Today

1. Contribute to employer retirement plans

If your company offers a retirement plan like a 401k or 403b plan, begin or increase your contributions to the plan. It is a great way to "pay yourself first" because the money is automatically deducted from your paycheck. In addition, a retirement plan like a 401k or 403b helps reduce your tax liability because the money is deducted from your paycheck pre-tax. For instance, if you earn $30,000 annually and you contribute 10% or $3,000 to your retirement plan, you pay taxes on an income of $27,000 instead of $30,000. Your contributions to your 401k/403b and any investment gains will not be taxed until you make a withdrawal from the plan (preferably at retirement and not before).

If your company has a matching program for the retirement plan, aim to contribute up to the company match so that you do not miss the "free" money your company is offering.

An example of a matching program is a company matching 50% of your contributions up to 6% of your salary. This means that on your $30,000 salary, when you contribute $1,800 (6% x $30,000), your company will contribute $900. If you contribute 3%, or $900, your company contributes only $450. You are missing an additional $450 in "free" money from your company.

Be sure to find out about the vesting period for your company. Vesting is the period before the company contributions belong to you 100%. Some companies have an immediate vesting period, while others have a vesting period of up to five years. Vesting periods vary from company to company.

The investments in 401k/403b plans are usually mutual funds. 401k/403b plans have a maximum annual contribution amount determined annually by the government and have age restrictions for penalty-free withdrawal. For 2014, the contribution limit for both 401k and 403b plans is $17,500 ($23,000 if you are 50 or older).

2. Open an Investment Retirement Account (IRA) account

The most common IRAs are traditional IRAs and Roth IRAs. The main difference is that a traditional IRA is funded with pre-tax dollars, similar to the 401k/403b retirement plans described earlier, while the Roth IRA is funded with after-tax dollars and earnings grow tax-free. For instance, if a contribution of $1,000 to your Roth IRA has grown to $5,000 by the time you withdraw it, the entire $5,000 can be withdrawn without paying taxes on the additional $4,000 if you meet the withdrawal criteria.

There are income limits that determine eligibility for contributing to an IRA, and age limits for penalty-free withdrawal. The 2014 max contribution for 2014 is $5,500 ($6,500 if you are 50 or older).

3. Open a Personal Investment Account

The previous investment accounts discussed were retirement accounts that provide tax advantages and have accompanying restrictions. A personal investment account, also called a taxable account, can be opened at any brokerage firm. You can trade different types of investments for a fee, and withdrawals from the account or closure of the account are at your discretion. Any dividends paid into the account are included in your income when you file your taxes, and any gains from the sale of your investment are subject to the capital gains tax when you file your taxes.

Online Brokerage Firms

Employer plans are maintained at Brokerage Firms of the employer's choosing, and you choose the Brokerage Firms of your choice when opening a personal investment account or IRA. Online brokerage firms tend to have lower trading fees, which is especially important when you first embark on your investing journey. There are many brokerage firms out there, including full-service ones that will provide you with a financial advisor. Be sure to select a firm that best meets your needs. Start by visiting each firm's website to learn more about them and their services.

To get you started, I have compiled a list of a few brokerage firms and developed a personalized "To Do" checklist for you.

Figure 16: Comparison of online Brokerage Firms (as of December 2014)

Brokerage Firm	Online Trades	Account Minimum
ShareBuilder	$6.95	None
E*Trade	$9.99	$500
Scottrade	$7.00	$500
TD Ameritrade	$9.99	None
Fidelity	$7.95	$2,500

CONCLUSION

- ❖ Start investing today and your future self will thank you.

- ❖ If you think you need a lot of money to begin investing, think again!

- ❖ Paying yourself first is the best way to ensure you keep investing.

- ❖ Automatic monthly investing is a great way to begin investing and continue to grow an investment portfolio.

- ❖ The earlier you begin investing the better because of the power of compounding.

- ❖ Be mindful of fees and expense ratios. They will reduce your ROI.

- ❖ There may be "free" money from your company; take advantage of your company's matching program and tax incentives from the government.

Visit my website **www.thefiwoman.com** for useful links, tools and my weekly blog.

"A good financial plan is a road map that shows us exactly how the choices we make today will affect our future"

- *Alexa Von Tobel, CEO of LearnVest*

Your Personal "To Do" Checklist

For Everyone

- ☑ Make a budget

- ☑ Determine how much you can set aside to invest and the frequency

Just starting out

- ☐ Participate in your company's 401(k) or 403(b).

- ☐ Research and select investments of your choice (You may want to start with Index funds or ETFs that track the S&P 500 and total bond market, using Expense Ratio as a selection criteria).

- ☑ Improve your knowledge by visiting my website **www.thefiwoman.com** for tips, useful links, and tools.

Already participate in a company retirement plan/Company doesn't offer a plan

- ☐ Open a traditional IRA or Roth IRA with a brokerage firm (Income restrictions and contribution limits apply)

☐ *Optional step: Open a personal investment account with a brokerage firm in addition to your Traditional or Roth IRA.*

☐ Link your bank account to your brokerage firm or direct deposit a portion of your paycheck.

☐ Research and select investments of your choice (You may want to start with Index funds or ETFs that track the S& 500 and total bond market, using Expense Ratio as a selection criteria).

☐ Set up automatic investments at a frequency of your choice (weekly, monthly, or quarterly).

☐ Improve your knowledge by visiting my website **www.fiwoman.com** for tips, useful links, and tools.

Prefer a Financial Advisor/Currently have one

☐ Schedule Quarterly meetings with your Financial Advisor to discuss your goals and options

☐ Improve your knowledge by visiting my website **www.fiwoman.com** for tips, useful links, and tools.

INDEX OF COMMONLY USED INVESTMENT AND STOCK MARKET TERMS

401(k)/403(b) Tax-advantaged employer sponsored retirement plans provided by Corporate and Government employers

Back End Load A sales charge is assessed at the time of selling a mutual fund

Bond A security issued by a company, government or agency in exchange for fixed payments, at a specified frequency, and for a specified length of time to the bondholder.

Bond Quote The amount or price an investor will pay for a bond expressed in relation to the face value

Bond Yield The return on a bond based on the price an investor paid for it

Brokerage Firm Firms that trade securities on behalf of clients. There are different types of Brokerage Firms

Coupon Also called the Coupon Rate is the interest rate on a bond when it is issued.

89

Coupon Frequency The frequency that interest from a bond is paid to the bondholder. Typically every six months, and is spelled out in the investment prospectus

Coupon Payment The interest payment that is paid to a bondholder. The amount and frequency depend on the Coupon Rate and Coupon Frequency.

CPI Consumer Price Index is a basket of stocks from various sectors of the economy. It is used to measure the health of the economy

Diversification An investing strategy to minimize investment risk. It involves investing in different types of stocks and not putting "your eggs in one basket"

Dividends Profit from a company that is shared with its shareholders. It is expressed as a per share amount.

EPS Earnings-per-share is the company's profit expressed in a per share amount. A company's EPS can be found on its income statement.

ETF Exchange Traded Fund consist of individual stocks or bonds, like Mutual Funds,

Ex-dividend Date The last day an investor can buy a stock and still receive a dividend payment.

Face-value or Par value The redeemable amount of a bond, typically $1000. It is the amount that is returned to the bond holder when the bond term ends.

Front End Load A sales charge is assessed at the time of buying a mutual fund.

Index Funds Mutual Funds or ETFs that track a stock market index.

IPO Initial Public Offering is when a company first makes its stock available to the public and begins trading in the stock market

Market Capitalization Calculated by multiplying a company's share price by its outstanding shares.

Mutual Funds A collection of individual stocks or bonds that provide investors with diversification.

NAV Net Asset Value of a Mutual Fund is the amount per share that an investor pays when buying the mutual fund. It is calculated at the end of every trading day.

No Load A mutual fund without a sales charge

OTC Over-the-counter refers to trading a stock that is not listed on one of the major stock exchanges

Outstanding Shares The number of shares issued by a company and in circulation in the stock market

P/E Price per earnings is calculated by dividing a stock's price by its EPS.

Roth IRA A tax advantaged retirement plan that allows contributions to grow tax free. Income, contribution and withdrawal restrictions apply.

Securities Investment instruments like stocks and bonds that are traded in the stock market.

Stock OwnershIssued by a company. Investors buy shares of stock and become owners of the company.

Stock Exchange A company such as the NYSE that handles the transactions involved with trading securities

Stock Market A place where securities are bought and sold

Stock Market Index A basket of stocks that is used to track stock market performance or performance of a sector. The Dow and S&P 500 are examples of indices.

Target Fund A mix of stock and bond mutual funds based on your planned year of retirement.

Traditional IRA A tax advantaged retirement plan that allows contributions to grow tax deferred. Income, contribution and withdrawal restrictions apply.

Vesting Period The amount of time that must elapse before an employee fully owns any contributions made by an employer to a retirement plan.

ABOUT THE AUTHOR

Ramat Oyetunji graduated from the University of Maine with an MBA in 2005. She is passionate about investing and has 15 years of experience investing in the stock market.

Her philosophy is that taking a simplified approach to investing, mixed in with a little bit of irreverence, will demystify the Stock Market and encourage more people to invest. By linking everyday images with investing concepts, readers remember and understand the concepts better and are likely to feel more confident about investing.

Final Thoughts

My Financial Goals are ....?

_____

_____

I Have Taken These Steps .....

_____

_____

The Challenges I'm Facing are ....

_____

_____

I Am Confident I Will Achieve My Financial
Goals because .....

_____

_____

I Am Celebrating These Financial
Milestones .....

_____

_____

CPSIA information can be obtained at www.ICGtesting.com
Printed in the USA
LVOW04s0619060315

429406LV00014BB/658/P